Kinsale Anthology

Edited by
Barry Moloney & Matthew Geden

Anam Press

Published July 2005 in a first edition of 1000 copies
Anam Press,
5 Friars Court,
Friars Street,
Kinsale,
Co. Cork,
Ireland
anampress@eircom.net

ISBN 0954302354

Published with the assistance of Kinsale Arts Week 2005

Cover image: *Old Kinsale* by Patrick Hennessy,
Crawford Art Gallery, Cork

Printed by Betaprint

Table of Contents

Poetry

James Clarence Mangan – Cean Salla	7
Thomas Davis – The Boatman of Kinsale	9
Aubrey de Vere – The March to Kinsale	11
Austin Clarke – The Marriage Night	13
Desmond O'Grady – Kinsale	15
Dún Chearmna	16
The Manuscripts of Louis MacNeice	18
John Montague – After Kinsale, 1604	20
Derek Mahon – Birdlife	21
On the Automation of the Irish Lights	22
Christmas in Kinsale	24
Kinsale	27
Matthew Geden – Ghost Story	28
Criose Brogan – Irish Exile	29
Afric Hamilton – The Discovery of Kinsale	30
Catriona Ryan – The Robin	31
Michael Hamburger – To a Fellow Poet	32
Gabriel Ezutah – Demands of Life	34

Prose

Lennox Robinson – from *Three Homes*	37
Robert Gibbings – from *Sweet Cork of Thee*	45
Maureen Murphy – from *A Child of Two Continents*	57
Aidan Higgins – from *Sodden Fields*	63
Rosemary Canavan – The Battle of Kinsale, from *Hugh*	73
Augustus Young – Tree Ring	80
Alannah Hopkin – The Sleakin Monument	89
Notes on the Authors	99
Acknowledgements	102

Poetry

Cean-Salla

The last words of Red Hugh on his departure from Ireland for Spain.

Weep not the brave dead;
Weep rather the living,
On them lies the curse
Of a doom unforgiving.
Each dark hour that rolls
Shall the memories they nurse,
Like molten hot lead
Burn into their souls –
A remorse long and sore,
They have helped to enthral a
Great land evermore,
They who fled from Cean-Salla.

Alas, for thee, slayer
Of the kings of the Norsemen,
Thou land of sharp swords
And strong kerns and swift horsemen.
Land ringing with song,
Land whose Abbots and Lords,
Whose heroic and fair
Through centuries long
Made each palace of thine
A new western Walhalla;

Thus to die without sign
On the field of Cean-Salla.

My ship cleaves the wave;
I depart for Iberia.
But, Oh with what grief
With how heavy and dreary
Sensation of ill
I should welcome a grave.
My career has been brief,
But I bow to God's will.
Yet if now all forlorn
In my green years I fall, a
Long exile I mourn,
But I mourn for Cean-Salla.

Thomas Davis

The Boatman of Kinsale

His kiss is sweet, his word is kind,
His love is rich to me;
I could not in a palace find,
A truer heart than he.
The eagle shelters not his nest
From hurricane and hail
More bravely than he guards my breast,
The boatman of Kinsale.

The wind that round the Fastnet sweeps
Is not a whit more pure –
The goat that down Cnoc Sheehy leaps
Has not a foot more sure.
No firmer hand nor freer eye
E'er faced an autumn gale –
De Courcey's heart is not so high
The boatman of Kinsale.

The brawling squires may heed him not,
The dainty stranger sneer,
But who will dare to hurt our cot
When Myles O'Hea is here?
The scarlet soldiers pass along;
They'd like, but fear, to rail;
His blood is hot, his blow is strong,
The boatman of Kinsale.

His hooker's in the Scilly van,
When seines are in the foam,
But money never made the man,
Nor wealth a happy home.
So blest with love and liberty,
While he can trim a sail,
He'll trust in God and cling to me,
The boatman of Kinsale.

Aubrey de Vere

The March to Kinsale

Decr., A.D. 1601.

O'er many a river bridged with ice,
Through many a vale with snow-drifts dumb;
Past quaking fen and precipice
The princes of the North are come.
Lo, these are they that year by year
Rolled back the tide of England's war:
Rejoice, Kinsale, thy help is near:
That wondrous winter march is o'er.
And thus they sang, "To-morrow's morn
Our eyes shall rest upon the foe;
Roll on, swift night, in silence borne;
And blow, thou breeze of sunrise, blow."

Blithe as a boy on marched the host
With droning pipe and clear-voiced harp;
At last above the southern coast
Rang out their war-steeds whinny sharp.
And up the sea-salt slopes they wound
And airs once more of ocean quaffed;
Those frosty woods the rocks that crowned,
As though May touched them, waved and laughed.
And thus they sang, "To-morrow's morn
Our eyes shall rest upon our foe;

Roll on, swift night, in silence borne;
And blow, thou breeze of sunrise, blow."

Beside their watch-fires couched all night
Some slept, some laughed, at cards some played.
While chaunting on a central height
Of moonlight crag, the priesthood prayed:
And some to sweetheart, some to wife,
Sent message kind while others told
Triumphant tales of recent fight,
Or legends of their sires of old,
And thus they sang:– "To-morrow's morn
Our eyes at last shall see the foe;
Roll on, swift night, in silence borne;
And blow, thou breeze of sunrise, blow."

Austin Clarke

The Marriage Night

O let her name be told
At dusk   while fishermen
Take nobles on the oar
And pass the fiery dice
Of wineshops at the harbour,
That flush them in the haze:
There is a darker town
Of ships upon the wave.

The morning she rode down
Where topsails, that had brought
A blessing from the Pope,
Were scrolled in early water:
Such light was on her cheekbone
And chin – who would not praise
In holy courts of Europe
The wonder of our days?

All saw in that cathedral
The great Earls kneel with her;
The open book was carried,
They got up at the gospel.
In joy the clergy prayed,
The white-clad acolytes
Were chaining, and unchaining,
Fire-hearted frankincense.

Upon her night of marriage,
Confessions were devout;
Murmuring, as religion
Flamed by, men saw her brow.
The Spaniards rolled with flag
And drum in quick relays;
Our nobles were encamping
Each day around Kinsale.

But in deceit of smoke
And fire, the spoilers came:
Tower and unmortar'd wall broke
Rich flight to street and gate.
O she has curbed her bright head
Upon the chancel rail
With shame, and by her side
Those heretics have lain.

Desmond O'Grady

Kinsale

Cúin tSaile or Ceann tSaile:
Quiet of the Sea or Head of the Ocean.
Either way, home-haven. Here we all
live blow-ins: exiles, or exiles from
exile. And we love our ease, our idleness.
You would too if you lived here among us.

The Bandon river finds sea exit here,
Atlantic spawning salmon entrance,
Kinsale origins flowered beyond the ice sphere
which makes Time and History a nonsense.
Here Celtic alternative order fought, died,
sixteen one; left us Ireland's modern divide.

We sleep side by side, together,
enjoying harmony's just measure
without weapons on display for war.

Dún Chearmna

Folamh anocht Dún Chearmna
do Ráith Teamhra is cúis bhaoghail;
méad uaigneasa an dúin dreachglain –
beart do bheartaibh an tsaoghail.

Ríoghradh fhial an dúin duasbhuig
ar nach bíodh uamhain foghla,
dá n-éis is truagh mar táimsi,
'sgan ann acht áite folmha.

Gearr go rabhad 'na n-uathadh,
Ráth Chruachan is Ráth Teamhra
gá beag dóibh so do robhadh? –
folamh anocht Dún Chearmna.

Dún Chearmna On The Old Head Of Kinsale

Dún Chearmna is empty tonight,
there are dangerous signals from Tara;
much loneliness in the clean-faced fort
from such great threat to life.

That hospitable fort of generous kings
was no empty cave,
now it is and pitied as I am,
with him gone it is an empty place.

Corncrakes sound plentiful in some places,
Rathcrogan and Tara ringforts,
do you need more warning?
Dun Chearmna is empty tonight.

Anon. (9-10th century)
Translated by Desmond O'Grady

The Manuscripts of Louis MacNeice

One surely tires eventually of the frequent references – the gossip,
the praise, the blame, the intimate anecdote – to those
who, for one unpredictable reason or another (living
abroad, difference of age, chance, the friends one chose,
being detained too long at the most opportune moment) one
never, face to tactile face, has met; but who,
had the way things fall fallen favourably, once met, for some
right psychic force, would have been polar, kindred you –
though time, space, human nature, sometimes contract
to force the action done that makes abstraction fact.

Here in this mock of a room which might have been yours, might have been
the place of our eventual meeting, I find a berth temporarily
(so long too late) among your possessions.
Alone, except for your face
in the framed photos, I sit, with your manuscripts spread over my knees,
reliving the unpublished truths of your autobiography.
On the shelves and table, desk, floor, your books
and papers, your bundles of letters – as if you were just moving in
or out, or had been already for years –
like a poem in the making you'll never now finish.

Through the windows I see down to the hook of Old Kinsale
Harbour.

Mid-summer. Under the sun the sea as smooth as a dish.
Below on the quays the fishermen wind up the morning's business:
stacking the fishboxes, scraping the scales from their tackle and
hands.
Behind this house the hills shovel down on the town's slate roofs
the mysterious green mounds of their history.
Flaming fir, clouted holly.
Not an Irish harbour at all, but some other –
the kind you might find along the Iberian coast, only greener.

Down to here, down to this clay of contact between us, Hugh O'Neill
once marched
from way up your part of the country, Ulster, the winter of sixteen
hundred and one, to connect with the long needed Spaniards three
months
under siege in the Harbour. Having played the English their own
game and watched
all his life for his moment, he lost our right lot in one bungled night
and with it the thousands of years of our past and our future.
He began what divides the North they brought your ash back to,
from the South I have left
for Rome – where O'Neill's buried exiled. And here, then, this
moment, late
as the day is (what matter your physical absence) I grow towards
your knowing,
towards the reassurance of life in mortality, the importance, the
value of dying.

John Montague

After Kinsale, 1604

A messenger from the Pale
Found the hunted rebel
Living, like a woodkerne,
In the wet meadows near
His broken coronation stone.
From Tullyhogue
He rides to Mellifont
To kneel for an hour
Before the Lord Deputy
'Most sorrowfully imploring'
Her Sacred Majesty,
Promising to abjure
'All barbarous custom'
His tribal title, O Niall.
Mountjoy embraces him
Omitting to mention
That the red-haired queen
He so reverently entreats
Is dead a week.

Derek Mahon

Birdlife

The gulls are out at the Old Head
where the *Lusitania* went down
so we make do with rooks instead
among the tiered roofs of the town.
The gulls are down among the fish,
raiding the trawlers at the quay;
crows pace among our spilt rubbish
staring ferociously at the sea.

On the Automation of the Irish Lights

We go to the lighthouse over a golf-course now,
not whins and heather as we used to do,
though we loved golf a generation ago
when it was old sticks and rain-sodden sand –
the sea breeze and first-morning-springy turf,
the dewy, liminal silence of the rough,
the little club-house with its tin roof,
steamers and lightships half a mile from land,
an old sea civilization; but now, unmanned,
the wave-washed granite and limestone towers stand
on the edge of space untouched by human hand,
a routine enlightenment, bright but abandoned.
So long from Alexandria to Fastnet and Hawaii,
to Rathlin, Baily, Kinsale, Mizen, Cape Clear.
These are the stars in the mud, the moth's desire,
the cosmic golf that guides us *ab aeterno*
to 'a little cottage with a light in the window';
like Ptolemy and Ussher the mind creates
its own universe with these co-ordinates
marked out by beacons of perpetual fire
from the centuries of monastic candle-power
to the new technologies and the solar glow –
we are star water; as above, below.
Think (i) of evening light and tower shadow,
the families living in the toy buildings there

beneath that generalized, impartial stare,
the children 'abstract, neutral and austere',
star-clustering summer dusk, a single bird;
and (ii) rock keepers. Imagine them off-shore
in their world of siren-song, kelpie and mermaid,
listening to the wind and the short-wave radio
and exercising as best they can in tiny
gardens above the sea. Think finally (iii)
of tower lights rising sheer out of the sea
where after gales a grumbling boulder knocks,
shaking the whole place, at igneous rocks.
Wind high among stars, solstice and equinox
will come and go unnoticed by human eye –
no more solitude, dark nights of the soul;
the new noisy knowledge replaces the midnight oil.
Now the ivory towers will be 'visitor centres'
visited mostly during the long winters
by sea-birds – gannet, puffin, kittiwake –
and their quartz lenses' own impersonal stroke.

Christmas in Kinsale

Beyond the branches he saw the roof of her hut shining against the galactic spawn.
Aidan Higgins, *Flotsam and Jetsam*

After the fairy lights in seaside lounge and bar
the night walk under a blustery Advent sky,
sidereal frost systems money will never buy,
one gull on a night wave, one polished star,
crane-light at the quayside, a dark harbour-mouth.
Stars in the spars, Spar closing, Quinnsworth
and Super Valu shut, the oracles are dumb,
the blow-ins drinking for the thirst to come
on the estuary we swam once like the Bosphorus,
moonlight on ripples like flecks of phosphorus,
pausing at mid-stream for a shooting star,
wild gas we transit, the crushed dirt and ice,
a heavenly multitude, rock-storms of space,
a circling camera, wandering screwdriver –
already rock stars have their names out there,
in post-obituary orbit for all time.
The young are slouching into Bethlehem
as zealots turn out for the millennium
on Sinai and Everest, Patmos and Ararat,
container bodies, gaze fixed on the night
for a roaring wind and the promised meteorite

of fire and brimstone; Druid and Jacobite
will be there watching for the swords of light,
the *aisling* and the dreamt apocalypse
between an earthquake and a solar eclipse.
… Wind-chimes this morning as in younger years
from the Church of Ireland and the Carmelite friars,
smoke rising like incense from a chimney-pot.
Once, angels on every branch, scribes in the trees,
'a continuous chorus of divine praise'.
Does history, exhausted, come full cycle?
It ended here at a previous *fin de siècle*
though leaving vestiges of a distant past
before Elizabeth and the Tudor conquest –
since when, four hundred years of solitude,
rainfall on bluebells in an autumn wood…
Holed up here in the cold gardens of the west
I take out at mid-morning my Christmas rubbish.
Sphere-music, the morning stars consort together
in a fine blaze of anticyclone weather
cradling the calm inner, the rough outer harbour,
the silence of frost and crow on telephone lines,
the wet and dry, the garbage and the trash,
remains of rib and chop, warm cinders, ash,
bags, boxes, bulbs, and batteries, bathroom waste,
carcases, tinfoil, leaves, crumbs, scraps and bones –
if this were summer there would be clouds of flies
buzzing for joy around the rubbish bins.

The harsh will dies here among snails and peonies,
its grave an iridescence in the sea-breeze,
a bucket of water where the rainbow ends.
Elsewhere the cutting edge, the tough cities,
the nuclear wind from Windscale, derelict zones;
here the triumph of carnival, rinds and skins,
mud-wrestling organisms in post-historical phase
and the fuzzy vegetable glow of origins.
A cock crows good-morning from an oil-drum
like a peacock on a rain barrel in Byzantium;
soap-bubbles foam in a drainpipe and life begins.
I dreamed last night of a blue Cycladic dawn,
again the white islands shouting, 'Come on; come on!'...

Kinsale

The kind of rain we knew is a thing of the past –
deep-delving, dark, deliberate you would say,
browsing on spire and bogland; but today
our sky-blue slates are steaming in the sun,
our yachts tinkling and dancing in the bay
like racehorses. We contemplate at last
shining windows, a future forbidden to no one.

Matthew Geden

Ghost Story

Don't snuff out that candle,
don't leave your room, try
to ignore the footsteps – the padding
in your life. You are only one small
step away from the horror film,
one giant leap from the dark.
Can you hear the soft rustle
of her nightgown, the creak of doors
as she passes through? Taste
the fear, the lump in your throat
when you know she's outside,
a lost soul in the corridor.
You are part of the T-house
mystery, you will never forget
the way she slid past, you will
want to hold her in your arms
like a secret but you'll lose her;
you don't have a ghost of a chance.

Criose Brogan

Irish Exile: From the play *Flight from Kinsale*

Clear slips the light,
Through the long sleeves of morning,
Rain grey and still,
Lone, a black little tree,
Glow upon glow
Lo, a headland dawning,
Gulls on a white screech
Bat in from the sea.

The rose and the yellow veils,
Softly appearing,
Glide up and are gone
To the blue drift of day,
Naked, our green land
Away to the old hills,
Open forever the innocent bay,

No man created this
Stretched out before me,
No man dictated
It should be this way,
Exile is nothing
This cannot be conquered
Brought low, or bartered,
Or given away.

Afric Hamilton

The Discovery of Kinsale

Lightning impulse guided our movements
as though migrations wind had flung an arrow
and, like coloured marbles rolling slopewards
we descended south, down winding roads and narrow
when suddenly below us, from the crest
grenaded to a spinning, sudden stop,
we burst upon a sight so latinesque
it exploded in kaleidoscopic rocks
of sapphire, ruby, pearled and coiled, a tail
quick-flicking lights across the evening silk
of sky-pink sea, tinkling masts and sails
quite soft-edged, dimming in twilight to milk

thus, blowing in, silent as dandelion heads
we were caught in Kinsale and never left.

Catriona Ryan

The Robin

The Kinsale landscape is winter bound
Mangled wires, pillowed bushes
Of snow clouds resting in the Robin's
Place of fire.

His eyes are worded sacrifice
For the old lady's offerings of
Bread:

"Cerunnos-sent totem logic,
Fire brand, wren-tempered breeze,
Little twitching, Cherry-breasted
Winter pain. Delicate presence,
All presence from the sun's bounty".

Her breast is filled with Bethlehem
Thorns. He flies through her
Old house, garden-walled, pure
Spirit of a doorless aesthetic.

The old lady's ghost sleeps in
The wooden walled deep-spade
Trailers of verse.

Her hands are palpable
And oak-filled.

Michael Hamburger

To a Fellow Poet
John Montague, for his sixtieth birthday

Well past the post that marked no hopes or fears
Because we run no race, but lap the years
Until we drop, and cannot win or lose,
Gasping I stammer out my lack of news:

Brain cells – or data stored by them – grow brittle.
How, then, connect, who recollect so little?
"Cork" and "Kinsale" I think, but see no place,
Mere aura, not the features of each face
Met there – or was it elsewhere? – as your guest.
But one thing, native to my East, your West,
Palpable, living, shifting, stays with me:
Your gift, tree lupin, carried from your sea
To mine, your garden to my garden, where
It thrives, indifferent to the harsher air;
By now self-seeded, intermarried, too,
With Russell hybrids, purple, pink or blue,
Into whose half-arborean offspring bees
Mixed its faint yellow shades, new subtleties;
(Here sexual surgery mutates no gene
For blossom bigger, gaudier, and obscene)
But more of its true, pallid, moon-cold kind
On small-leaved stalks that straggle, sprawl or wind.

Poems are less transplantable. They draw
On local nutrients, obey a law
Not universal, though to common skies
From their peculiar darknesses they rise.

So out of our long silence, distant friend,
Cut flowers at best, these token rhymes I send
Which, rootless, hardly will outlast the day –
Their function not to be but to convey
Remembered continuities that are all
The running leaves the runners till they fall
Or only pause, drop out beside the track
To breathe unstrained and let the strings go slack.

Such rest between long labours I wish you,
Growth, like your gift's, the circling years renew,
Such wisdom as we need to suffer age
While true to our folly, still we love and rage.

Gabriel Ezutah

Demands of Life

We may rave like trucks or cry like hawks,
We may crow like cocks or stand like rocks,
When life asks for change, for that next step.

We may stand and shake, shivering agape,
We may run like hares, from brave tigers,
How we kneel and beg like poor beggars!

As the sea moves on, the banks adjust,
As the winds push on, palms bend with trust,
The wise downward brook rejoins the sea,
As the wind-blown smoke goes home with glee.

All the pains of life, both big and small,
From wants to cancer, to homeward call,
Are to shape the soul, with light and love:
Life nev'r asks for more than we can give!

Prose

Lennox Robinson

Extract from *Three Homes* by Lennox Robinson, Tom Robinson and Nora Dorman

Through the wet warm January day the waggonette lumbered on, Wolf running gamely by its side his petticoats getting muddier and muddier. Jumbo occasionally trotted for a half-mile but spent most of the journey clambering affectionately from lap to lap. Nimrod in his basket ceaselessly complained. Dusk fell and it was late afternoon before we stopped in front of a hall-door in a narrow street. It was Fisher Street, Kinsale, the number of the house was five. Number five Fisher Street shared with six and seven a piece of ground behind them separating them from the quay. There was first a patch of grass, then a tennis-court, then a small garden divided between number five and number six. Beyond the garden a large gate gave on to the quay and beyond the quay was, of course, the sea. The tennis-court and the garden were reclaimed slob-lands and beside our garden was a waste of mud which filled up with water for a short time every twelve hours. It was a landlocked, desolate little expanse which had only subterranean connection with the sea, but a flat-bottomed boat lived in it (for the purpose of retrieving tennis-balls) and small crabs could be caught by fishing from our garden wall. The soil in the garden was shallow and poor, very different from the rich deep soil of Westgrove and the plants and bulbs my Mother imported dwindled and died, and the privet hedge which divided our patch from that of number six sucked the good out of the ground. I still can never see or smell privet without a feeling of vague hostility. Yet there were compensations in the shallow soil and in the unshadiness of the patch, tomatoes ripened well and I learned the pleasure of warm tomatoes, occasionally stolen and guiltily eaten.

 Doctor Dorman, our landlord, was, from the first moment that I recollect him a very old man who had retired from practice. Small, and dressed in shiny black clothes, he was kind to us children in a sort of way, but he was always a little terrifying. He was, after all, the landlord, the person who descended on the house from time to time in a fury because the roof leaked or the plumbing went wrong, the W.C. wouldn't function, the pipe was found choked by a bunch of withered flowers. Who had put them there? Why? Did we not know? The whole house was sunk in shame for twenty-four hours. He had two daughters, Avis and Dysie. The latter's real name was Diana. Avis was the grave elder sister, Dysie was young and dashing. She must have been past her first youth when I first knew her but she was extraordinarily energetic. She was a fierce and efficient tennis-player and served over-hand, a thing not generally done by lady players forty years ago. She had a curious method of service, she held the racket firmly a few inches from her face, through it she glared for fully twenty seconds and then she smote the ball. Perhaps the service was not so very deadly but the glare was intimidating and she had the reputation of being a very good player. Her style of playing suited the fashion of the day, a hard sailor-hat bristling with large hat-pins, a dark skirt and a light-coloured blouse with leg-of-mutton sleeves. Avis affected innocuous croquet. In the distant background – was it India or Aldershot? – hovered a brother in the R.A.M.C. He was quite distinguished, a charming man with a very elegant wife – Cassie. He was for many years a Colonel, later a General. The sisters were very proud of him. " My brother the Colonel," " My brother the General " – these phrases rang out loudly at tea-parties. The old doctor was deaf and the daughters as years went on became more and more loud-voiced. Quale Penrose, befogged in a yacht close to the Lower Road, sailed home safely to his moorings guided by the voices of the Miss Dormans who were walking on that road. They were whole-hearted Kinsalites. They occasionally went to Cork but seldom or never to Dublin and I am sure they had never been outside Ireland. If they had it was but to despise any place other than Kinsale which was clearly the centre of the universe. Years later when we were about to leave Kinsale, Dysie met me in the garden. It was the evening of the day that offered me release from purgatory. She said: "I am sure you are very sorry to be leaving," and I, rude child of thirteen, said: "No, I am very glad." She shrank as if I had struck her, declared I was very ungrateful and left me feeling myself a clumsy brute.

The town itself was strange. Kinsale is one of the rare Irish country towns which has an individuality and beauty of its own. It has changed much since I knew it first, many of the old houses with their large bow-windows have disappeared but the narrow winding streets still remain. Gentlemen's houses were side by side with shops or small houses, and a street which seemed almost a slum would suddenly display a large house and behind that house would stretch a very large garden crammed with fruit trees. When I read some story by Balzac of provincial life with its minute description of house and courtyard and garden I am always reminded of Kinsale. The grand houses in Kinsale, indeed, had no courtyards, they, opened immediately on to the broken pavement of the street but inside they generally had an eighteenth-century spaciousness though I cannot remember any that possessed remnants of fine eighteenth-century workmanship – mantelpieces, ceilings, or the like. The town falls steeply into the sea and the railway station and the military barracks stood outside on the top of a hill. The station could be approached either by Break-heart Hill, or, a shorter route, Feather-bed Lane, called so in irony I suppose for never was there a pathway so filled with loose stones. It was a satisfaction to us children to know that a commercial traveller hurrying for a train had dropped dead on Break-heart Hill.

Number five, though smaller than its neighbour, was a commodious house, three storeys high on the street side, four storeys on the garden side. On the right as you entered was the study, at the back a large dining-room. The floor above contained a long double drawing-room with three windows looking over the street and at the back, corresponding to the dining-room was a bedroom used by my Father and Mother. On the top floor were other bedrooms. We four boys slept in the largest, in separate beds, the small room in the middle was the Governess's – Miss Lewis – the end one was Nora's. There was also a W.C., and on the back side of the house the servants' bedroom. It had the queer stuffy smell that all servants' rooms have.

We had brought our own furniture from Westgrove and the house was well furnished. A few pieces were really beautiful and old and nearly all of it was sound. The drawing-room was quite elegant. It was the period of Liberty decoration and artyness, so there was an oriental corner hung with tapestries and there was a little oriental lamp suspended from the ceiling by chains. It used to be lighted in the winter on Tuesday afternoons when my Mother was "at home" to the society of Kinsale. She trailed her country-house elegance into Fisher Street and was only slowly broken into being a curate's wife with a family of five children and an income of one hundred and fifty pounds a year. She used to receive her guests in a tea-gown. She had two tea-gowns, one was of dark-red silk, the other of some lighter, buff-coloured stuff trimmed with fur. Both were very beautiful, the fur one was the less beautiful but it had fur. If only the other one had had fur it would have been superb. Possibly her elegance and her attempt at a salon were a little absurd, and probably Kinsale gossiped and laughed – but I am sure not unkindly. My Mother wasn't a fool, she was sentimental but exceedingly intelligent and very kind. "At-home days" abounded in Kinsale. It was quite difficult to remember whose was "the first Wednesday" and whose "the third Friday," they gave rise to small and harmless jealousies. Afternoon tea on my Mother's Tuesdays was quite an affair. The beautiful cakes were always home-made, for only the most slovenly households had "bought" cakes – Although an exception was made in the case of cakes baked by the Miss Orrs. The Miss Orrs had a small bakery and were known to everyone. Miss Maddy Orr played the organ in St Multose church, Miss Harrie gave violin lessons and the eldest – I forget her name – made the cakes. Such cakes could hardly be considered shop cakes, they were certainly in a different category to the cakes of Jacob and Co., indeed hardly a tea-party and certainly no summer picnic was complete without one of Miss Orr's jam-sandwiches. As well as the home-made cakes – handed round on three-tiered cake-stands – there were plates of hot toast and bread and butter served in tight rolls. I think this last was a speciality introduced by our governess, Miss Lewis, and probably learned from the pages of *Home Chat*, a magazine which was bought and read every week. You needed for the rolls the very freshest bread cut very thin and liberally buttered, and fresh bread can only be cut thin by using a very sharp knife and one kept hot by being constantly plunged into boiling water. The result was delicious and we used to wait, we children, peering over the banisters until the last guest had gone and then swoop into the drawing-room to devour the remains of the tea. The tea was served in beautiful and valuable china cups which were washed afterwards by my Mother. She would not trust them to a servant.

Robert Gibbings

Extract from *Sweet Cork of Thee*

Kinsale is like an ancient oak forest whose topmost shoots have suffered with the years but whose roots are deep into the soil, and whose trunks and branches, rich with ferns and flowers and mosses, will never lose their character.

The town, whose first charter was granted by Edward III in 1333, stands at the head of an extensive harbour, encompassed by hills. Its houses are built along those hills, one above the other, so that there seems scarcely a basement that does not overlook an attic. No two houses are alike and it may be for that reason that their occupants also have an individuality of character. The town straggles and climbs. There are main streets in which two men on bicycles can scarcely pass. There are thoroughfares that for steps rival the Strada Stretta of Malta. And on all sides there are ruins of forts and castles: James Fort, 1601, a keep within its moat on the hill, and Charles Fort, 1670, whose bastions meet the water's edge, the two of them guarding the narrows between outer and inner harbours. There is a block house that once assisted the forts, and a mile or so up the River Bandon, which flows into the harbour, there is Ringroan Castle, not to mention many others. It is on record that after the Battle of Kinsale in 1601, the officers and men of Queen Elizabeth's army, to commemorate their victory over the Spanish troops, subscribed £700 to purchase books for the library of Trinity College Dublin, which speaks well for the military of that time. Visitors to Trinity College will find over the stairs leading to the library a large painting of the Battle of Kinsale with an inscription concerning its special significance in that position.

Ringroan Castle, which belongs to the de Courcys, Lords Kingsale, is thought to have been built by them in the thirteenth century. With the nearby James Fort it was the scene of the last Williamite battle in Ireland, in September 1690. Nothing of that castle remains today but a single wall, standing like a great monolith on the hill. Fifty years ago there was another wall surviving. I remember it because it was there that, at the age of ten, I made my first attempt at sketching. With another boy, now a Very Revd., I crept away shyly, complete with notebook and pencil, and later in the day was not displeased by my parents' comments when I ventured to show them what I had done. This was my first practical adventure into the realms of art, though a year earlier when on holiday at Baltimore, a sea port some fifty miles from Kinsale, my eyes had been opened by a friend of my mother's who could do what seemed to me wonders with a box of water-colours. She must have been about thirty-five years of age and I was about nine, and I used to stand behind her for hours while she sketched, watching the miracles she worked on paper, watching too, the lights in the rather prim coils of her flaxen hair. I confessed to my mother that I would like to marry Emily, but she gently dissuaded me.

I do not remember any other great excursions into art at that time. My energies were too taken up in shivering at early morning bathing parties and sweating at midday bicycle picnics, for I was the youngest among my companions and I found it very hard to keep up with them.

At that time Kinsale was a prosperous town. Fishing boats from Scotland, Cornwall and the Isle of Man followed the herring and the mackerel in their courses, and during the week the quay would be alive with men and women salting and packing the fish, while at the week-end the inner harbour would be solid with smacks. At that time, too, a British regiment stationed in the town brought a considerable revenue to the business community. Now the fish have changed their feeding-grounds and the troops have departed, and the town has gone quietly and peacefully to sleep.

'Ah, but isn't it grand to be together again, after all the troubles?' said an elderly woman to me on Denis's Quay. 'Yerra, never mind the barracks. Sure, it brought great money to some, but what good was it to others? And what harm is it, too, if the fishing is gone? 'Tis a pity, surely, but no matter. D'you remember the way we'd walk across the harbour on the decks of the smacks? 'Twas PL this and PL that, from Peel in the Isle of Man, and they'd be anchored over by the Lower Road. They'd be the first to arrive in March for the mackerel fishing, and then the Scotch boats would come for the herring in May, and they'd anchor beyond by the pier, and the Cornish boats would be in in August for the harvest mackerel. 'Tis over at the Scilly Dam some of them would be, and they had PZ on their bows for Penzance, or maybe SS for St. Ives, I think. And now the harbour is empty. Three lobster boats at the pier head and what would they get – maybe a few dozen of a night. And all the gentry are going or gone. Well, I suppose no man can live for ever. Sure, the old general above on the hill was ninety-three when he went, and the captain below in the town was eighty-seven. But tell me, isn't it a lovely harbour? Did you ever see nicer in all your travels? No! I'm thinking you never did. There's some visitors be talking of the smell at low tide but what's a bit of a smell. Sure 'tis only from the mud and what would mud be if it hadn't a bit of a smell. And don't I know and don't you know many the fine hearty man and girl was brought up on those smells, and, sure, isn't it all washed by the sea twice every day, and how could it do harm. There was a priest came here last year, from Italy he was, and, says he, there's no tides in the ocean around Italy at all, and when he seen the tide go out and leave the mud all bare, and then the tide to come in again and flood up to the doors of the houses without ever entering in: "Isn't it wonderful," says he, "the law and order of the Almighty?"'

We were standing on the edge of the quay, and before us was as nice a stretch of aromatic slob as you could ask to see or smell. Slime-covered ropes, chains, and cables led to half-sunken anchors or to yachts and row-boats lying on the worm-blistered mud. But the tide was rising and soon the same landscape would be transformed, its sheltered waters reflecting the erratic architecture of the town.

I had only fifty yards to walk to the house of an old friend, now a retired admiral. The bell wouldn't ring, the knocker seemed to have no effect on the household. The hall door was wide open, and I could have walked off with a pair of silver candelabra. Instead, I used the knocker a second time, more forcibly. The only reply was the opening of a window above my head. As I hadn't seen the admiral for forty years, and had never met 'his lady,' I didn't look up. Next moment a girl came hurtling down the stairs. She might have been the aunt of hers with whom I was in love at the age of twelve.

'Come in, come in!' she said. 'I'm father's daughter.'

'But you don't know who I am,' I said.

'I do,' she said.

'I put my head out of the window and I said to mother: "There's a man below at the door." "It's Bob Gibbings, " she said.'

'How did she know?' I asked.

'She's like that,' said the daughter.

At that moment her mother sailed in looking not unlike a stately ship that had weathered a storm. Her clothes were in ribbons. I was only conscious of shreds and streamers held together with pins and tackings of white thread.

'Pat is fitting me with a new dress,' she said.

The admiral appeared soon after, and he was followed by others of the family. We discussed old times in Kinsale, the model yacht regatta which my mother organized each year for the young people, and the Saturday night prayer meetings which my father organized when the fishing fleets were in the harbour. There was one old man at those meetings who always prayed. He invariably sat as far back in the hall as he could, until inspiration came: then he would move into the central aisle, drop on his knees, and begin to pray in a reverberating voice which steadily increased in volume. As he spoke he would work his arms backwards and forwards with a breast-stroke swimming action and while he did so he would be slowly moving forward on his knees. We boys knew that there would be no release until he met the platform. 'Tell me,' said the admiral, 'why was it your father didn't like the idea of becoming an artist?'

'Naked women,' I said. 'He thought I'd have to spend the rest of my life among them.' and then I told him how, years later, when the studio reproduced a few of my engravings, I sent a copy of the magazine to my sister. 'Merciful Heaven!' she said when she opened it. 'There's a girl with nothing on.' 'Oh my, my,' said my father. 'What will the poor boy come to?'

From the admiral I went to see Miss Harrie Orr who had

given me my very first lessons in drawing. 'Why, Bobby darling! is that yourself?' she said, throwing her arms round me and kissing me. We talked of my early efforts to copy geometric patterns, and of the school upstairs run by her sister Miss Eleanor, and then the subject changed to the old ladies who refused to bathe from the same beach as myself and my brother – 'great big boys of ten and twelve,' and thence to the girl who swam across the harbour with a shoal of porpoises gambolling near, and from her to the two girls who always played hockey in dresses with long trains. Finally of the spinster to whom my mother lent the rectory while we were on holiday. With the house and garden was also lent my pet duck, but when I got home after a month's absence there was no sign of Winnie. I was told that she had 'died.'

'Now,' said Harrie when I was leaving, 'Go down to the Castle Bar, 'tis no more than a few steps, and say a word to Mrs. Coleman. She remembers you.'

'If it isn't Bobby Gibbings himself,' said Mrs. Coleman from behind the bar as I went in. 'You don't remember me?' she said. 'But didn't I teach you your sums on a slate! Sure, I was Nora Crowley then, and I helped Miss Eleanor with her school.'

'Would you be any relation of Commander Gibbings?' asked a fisherman who was standing by the counter.

'A brother, probably,' I said.

'He commanded my ship in the first war, and faith when he heard I came from Kinsale I couldn't go wrong. When you see him tell him McCarthy was asking for him. Tell him I was in the last war, and tell him I was in the Merchant Navy in between wars and now I'm fishing – netting for salmon. I lost two of my sons in the last war,' he added.

Another fisherman dropped in. 'Torpedo,' they called him – 'Torpedo Tim.' he had been a bar steward in a cross-channel service during the first war and three times his ship had been sunk. When it happened for the third time, the crash came as he was locking up for the night. 'Got us again!' he muttered to himself. So he pulled out the till, stuffed the whole of its contents into his trousers pockets, and rushed on deck just as the ship took a lurch and sank. He hadn't had time to fasten his lifebelt and as he went down it hit him under the jaw, breaking most of his teeth. 'I came up spitting blood and teeth – I hadn't a tooth left in me head. I haven't one now,' he told me.

After he had been picked up and landed he was sent to hospital where they wanted to undress him and put him to bed. Not very likely! Nobody was going to take those trousers from him. Oh, very well, if he didn't want to go to bed he could go home, they said. So he was sent home, and the first thing his wife wanted to do was to put her poor shipwrecked mariner to bed. Again the value of these trousers recurred to him. 'He's gone queer in the brain with the blast,' said his wife. Not until he had the money safely hidden did he recover his sanity.

Next day I couldn't resist a visit to Thuillier's boat-building yard. As a boy I used to watch racing yachts growing out of a foam of shavings on his father's pier; as a young man I used to hire yachts from him for a couple of shillings a day. Now there was no sign of sail-cloth, masts, or spars, but a brand-new dinghy rested on the grass awaiting its owner. In the shed alongside the pier another dinghy was in the course of construction, many of its copper nails not yet riveted. Behind its newly planed, shining timbers of spruce there lay at the back of the shed an ancient bicycle – 'A boneshaker made by my father in '69,' said Mr. Thuillier. 'He modelled it in wood and then he took it along to Taed Murphy the blacksmith for the iron. Seventy-five pounds the whole thing weighed. But look at these, he said, pointing to two 'penny-farthings' thrown in a corner. 'We got them from the police; they tried them for a time but they were too conspicuous. Sure, a helmet on the top of one of them would be seen for miles. But they were lovely things to ride; they'd just glide off a stone if you met one. It was a beautiful sensation.'

Kinsale has produced many celebrated people, from Anne Bonny the pirate queen downwards. One gentleman of whom I have not spoken is Patrick Cotter O'Brien the giant, who was born in the neighbourhood in the year 1761. He died in Bristol at the age of forty-seven and was buried in the crypt of St. Joseph's Church in that city. As a boy, Cotter O'Brien was apprenticed to a stonemason, but he soon began to specialise in plastering ceilings, which thanks to his height he could do without the help of ladders. But a sudden change in his career occurred at the age of eighteen when a travelling showman agreed to pay his parents fifty pounds a year for his 'use.' There is no record of what Cotter was to get out of the bargain, but we may infer that it was limited, for it wasn't long before he left the showman and set up in a similar business on his own. By this time his imagination seems to have been in no way inferior to his physique, for on one of his handbills is printed:

'Just arrived in town, and to be seen in a commodious room at No. 11 Haymarket, nearly opposite the Opera House, the celebrated Irish Giant, Mr. O'Brien of the Kingdom of Ireland, indisputably the tallest man ever shown. He is a lineal descendant of the old puissant King Brien Boreau, and has in person and appearance all the similitude of that great and grand Potentate. It is remarkable of this family that however various the revolutions in point of fortune and alliance, the lineal descendants thereof have been favoured by Providence with the original size and stature which have been so peculiar to their family. The Gentleman alluded to measures near nine feet high.

ADMITTANCE ONE SHILLING.'

He forgot to mention that his immediate forbears in Kinsale were of normal size. However, his finger ring of gold, measuring one inch and a quarter in diameter and bearing many devices, was in the possession of a friend of mine, the late Henry Daunt of Kinsale, to whose granduncle in Bristol it had been given by O'Brien; and one of the giant's shoes, fifteen and a half inches in length, is to be seen in the Kinsale Museum.

Maureen Murphy

Extract from A Child of Two Continents

Going to church from Sandy Cove was always an important event. As each Sunday dawned, the horizon and the skies would be carefully scanned. Could we go by boat? Well, what was the glass doing? After the manner of most barometers, it was probably falling. With a family of three small children, it was very tempting to go by boat. Transport was thereby assured to a point within ten minutes' walk of the church itself, but – would the weather hold? If going by boat was out of the question, we would be faced with a two mile walk to the ferry, followed by a crossing of the wide, swiftly flowing Bandon River. The ferry boat, which was enormous and very ancient, would be crowded with women in their black Kinsale cloaks with hoods over their heads, and the men dressed in their best clothes, ready for Mass. The fare was tuppence return per head. One passenger would volunteer to pull the second oar for the ferryman. This was just as well because he, like his boat, was ancient. The boat, with its gunwale not more than a few inches clear of the water was headed up river to counteract the inevitable drift towards the harbour caused by the strong current. Thus, travelling more or less sideways like a crab, it would arrive at the slip exactly opposite the place where we had embarked.

Since the ferry boat was really catering for the crowd going to "Twelve Mass," and since our church service was at 11.30 a.m. we were apt to be late. The walk from the ferry was another quarter of an hour. It had, moreover, to be accomplished with children who were cross and dragging their feet, because by this time they did not want to go to church at all. The donning of best suits and clean frocks, hats and proper socks and shoes was an ordeal, after spending the whole week in old clothes and sand shoes through which usually peeped one or more toes.

It was hard enough to keep clean walking and going in the ferry boat. It was much more difficult when travelling in our own boat, with the extra hazards of splashes or indeed, rain itself. Still, as compensation, there were more things to look at. Sandy Cove Point was always interesting. Apart from the variability of the sea, the rocks were always lined with gulls, cormorants and puffins, sitting in rows and staring at us. They always looked so serious and pious, that I decided that they must be indulging in their own private devotions.

Once round Sandy Cove Point, we would head for

Money Point, avoiding the Farmer Rock with its little black buoy bobbing over it. Then, from Money Point, we would steer for Barley Cove, to keep ourselves out of the strong current of the Outer Harbour. From Barley Cove we would set our course straight for the Block House. On our way we passed that picnic place, so beloved of all the Dorman clan except us, called The Platters and Dishes. This had got its name from the curious rock formation which made a series of flat platforms. We would also pass the place where, during the Battle of Kinsale in the early seventeenth century, one end of the boom protecting the harbour had been attached. Round The Block House we would hug the shore as closely as possible, passing under James Fort. Then, facing the current, there would be a final spurt as we headed straight across the inner harbour to reach whichever quay had sufficient water, depending on the state of the tide. Most of us would alight there and set off for the church. Daddy and Jack would take the boat across the small stretch of water to the Raffeen moorings. To leave the boat at the slip was not always advisable. In a falling tide we would be likely on our return to find it aground in the mud.

St Multose Church is a twelfth century edifice with a square Norman tower. Over one of the entrance doors there is a little carving in stone of St Multose himself. At either side of the same doorway, there are deep cuts in the stonework which have been attributed to Cromwell's soldiers sharpening their swords. Inside the door, in the porch, there is a set of stocks in good condition. There are many interesting monuments and plaques. Also the royal arms and five hatchments, all dating from the seventeenth century. There are some beautiful stained glass windows, a number of which have been erected to members of our family. Daddy had planned to install one of these in memory of Mummy after she died but, since he himself died five months later, it could not be completed in time. The plaque bears their joint names together with that of Mummy's brother, Lennox Robinson who was a playwright and producer and a director of the Abbey Theatre in Dublin. Later, after Eileen's death, Jack and I added her name to the window but on a separate brass plate.

In those early years in Sandy Cove, the real ordeal of Sunday came after church. In response to a royal command from Daddy's step-mother, Grandma, we must all have dinner at Raffeen. Mummy hated a big mid-day meal, and Sunday dinner in Raffeen was indeed solid. I remember only boiled pig's cheek with boiled cabbage and masses of boiled potatoes, but perhaps it varied. The puddings were also very solid and designed to keep the diners satisfied for a long time. During the meal we would anxiously watch the weather and, if the wind seemed to be rising, Daddy would urge us into the boat as soon as possible, to start the homeward journey. This time we would be able to enjoy ourselves because hats, socks and shoes could be discarded and, if your frock got wet or dirty, it was of little consequence. Often, too, there was more excitement. The wind would be stronger and the waves bigger and the clop clop of the bow of the boat, as it bounced over the waves, would have increased. Sometimes it was decided that the boat should be lightened to go round Sandy Cove Point. Some of us would then be landed at Barley Cove and from there we would walk home. A crew of three would continue, often having to row quite far out into the bay in order to get into such a position that the big rollers would be directly astern and thus wash the boat past the point. From there on the island would give shelter and the rest of the journey would be accomplished easily. If conditions were very unfavourable, the boat had to return to Kinsale Harbour to be left there, and everybody came home by the ferry. In really stormy weather, the ferry itself might not be negotiable. In that case, there would be a seven mile walk to Kinsale, so church was really out of the question.

Aidan Higgins

An Extract from *Sodden Fields*

1987 Battle and Aftermath; the Beast of Ballynagrumoolia

If the wholesale slaughter that was the Battle of Kinsale finished off the rough princely world of Latinists and gallowglasses in three hours in the Ballinamona bog, had it not been lost already when McMahon sold out O'Neill in return for a bottle of the hard stuff on that miserable wet late December day 387 years ago? No?

Neap tides flooded 9,288 times into Ballymacus Creek where as a difficult thing you liked to retire, to sulk. Our independence won with jigs and reels God knows how many church collections later, and the national flag raised jerkily aloft in mismatching shades of dandelion orange (leaves, stalk and root containing a bitter milky juice) and septic green, divided by neutral white, and complemented by a National Anthem that was never any great shakes, 'composed' by a north Dublin house painter, a bowsy by the name of Carney reputedly related to the roistering Behans.

Years later, out walking with you on another soft December day beyond the ramparts, we spotted the Beast of Ballynagrumoolia beyond a denuded winter hedge. Pale and plump, the deep-set piggish eyes red-rimmed like an anus, the flaccid cheeks soiled with mud, immemorial slobber, shit and tears. The Beast's stiff yellow hair was erupting from under nodding headgear, fore-hooves rooting in the driveway, the twin enraged nostrils aflare; while from the deep barrel chest stormily rising and subsiding came grievous sighs and the most heartfelt groans. Great sods of earth were being hurled about; an apparition as alarming as a she-gorilla enraged – the very stuff of nightmares.

Scavengers, looters and pillagers, the extreme poor ofrey to cover the battlefields now become graveyards, a thousand of O'Neill's and O'Donnell's men become shades, in an unforgettable day that would be for Ireland what Kossovo would be for Hungary. But the poison was already being prepared and the wild geese scattered, soon to become extinct. Something was broken so that something else could begin.

And sure enough, scarcely had a year passed than there came yet another in the long roster of our betrayal; this one by the name of Jamsey Blake, turncoat and native of Galway who was said to be in the pay of Sir George Carew the Lord High President of Munster. It was he who arranged that poison be laid out for Red Hugh at a dinner in Simancas, watched him sample wine of the Palomino grapes, swig and swallow; take percebes, which are goose barnacles, now stuffed with death, take his portion with a slow easy hand. Blake, hidden, watched, and so did some ruffed and bearded Spanish grandees, not comprehending; saw him swallow it in a place now outside of time, wiped out by time, frozen within time.

As the Scots troops crouched miserably all night in cornstooks in freezing rain, their powder damp, their spirits low, awaiting Cromwell's fearful attack at sunup, time stopped. At daybreak the Scots troops began shuffling into line.

Elsewhere in other times and places in different darkness St Elmo's fire was glinting on damp Irish lances (not to be used much that day) and Panzer tank engines coughing into life at sunup were rolling toward Kusk. These fields, Kossovo and its crows, the tank battle of Kusk, the graveyard of Kinsale, a drenched cornfield in Scotland. Jamais deux sans trois; never four without more.

Shrapnel tore through the grey insentient air, bees with their hives knocked over. From the enemy lines the machine-gun fire was reaching out, stuttering, probing, stitching the air. Somewhere in the murk ahead lay the pierced barbed-wire entanglements. Juss trod on something soft and yielding – flayed human flesh not yet dead, himself dragged along by the current of time. His face felt stiff as a death mask, from generous tots of three-star Hennessy. The thought flew unsoberly through his head: Schicksal had become Schnicksal, both British and Germanic destiny become ridiculous and dirty, become piercing red-hot. The ordinary expectation of suffering was one thing; this was something else again.

The Beast of Ballynagrumoolia had come via Ballinspittle through all the intervening gardens of Munster, breaking down clapboard fences, trampling vegetable patches, grunting and sweating, to Kippagh.

The Battle of Kinsale was fought and lost one vile wet Sunday on 24 December 1601 and over in barely three hours. Within a period so brief a large force was destroyed by a smaller one, the English horse under Wingfield pursued the fleeing Irish as far as Innishannon five miles distant, killing at will. The Spanish presence within the town had been more a hindrance than a help. Trust not foreign friends; the old adage had a cruel ethnic twist to it. The River Bandon snaked about the small port, a walled town of 200 houses, as duodenum and colon, lower bowel and anus. Spared the shame of defeat, the Spanish were flushed down the river and out to sea. Don Juan del Aquila was in command. The Armada had sunk only thirteen years before. For the Irish, crippling defeats at the Yellow Ford and Benburb, and now Kinsale, the final setback. The ancestors had begun to seem strange. Kolkrabe the Raven greets you! Shaking out sodden feathers, stropping its beak on the bars of the cage. Hiding its food, first under this stone, then under that. Swearing profusely, e'er all be over and done with. Ever since the sixteen century the wind had been blowing against European Catholicism.

Our Jamesie O'Connor, a fifth- or sixth-generation bachelor, on the dole, impoverished and half-mad, was as a lost creature struggling in a mangrove swamp. Still believing that his dead brother had been converted into a crow and Jamsie out after him in all weathers in a long unchanged greasy overcoat in one pocket of which he kept his silent gun – a catapult.

He dwelt bachelor-style in a cramped and fetid one-room Assumption Terrace cottage hard by the charitable fishmongers who fed him, opposite the health centre

('Pregnant? We can help') and the Garda station out of which at any moment the opera-loving but ill-tempered Guard Con Concannon might purposefully stride, demanding a licence for the silent gun, make him eat crow. Insects too have their hour.

Jamesie's window overlooked the end of the ancient Celtic world. He whittled at odds and ends to make a fire, kept a mangy cat, preferred candles to newfangled notions such as electric light, drank in the Harp and Shamrock, where he was known as 'Whackers'. As with Wagner before him, he suffered agonies from skin disease, piles and rotten bladder, his memory shot to pieces, Irish to the core, his temper uncertain, he wanted to kill the crow that was his brother. The same old dingdong.

Out walking in winter, one memorable evening, we encountered the Beast of Ballynagrumoolia at close quarters, in all her glory. A dinted and holed aluminium chamber-pot was clamped down on the pointed skull and fastened with a demi-veil of fishing net knotted about the throat in a loose fashion with brown scapulars contesting with an Immaculate Conception badge on a faded crimson thread; the white paint cracked on the chamber, the blue rim chipped, and strapped about it (a daring touch) welder's goggles. A scarf of pale green fruit-netting the colour of a well-weathered copper church dome bisected the neck. And from neck to ankle a kimono-like vestment of a nondescript dull colour, a swaggered double skirt like a priest's cassock or Franciscan's habit, at midriff a double length of hairy twine, of the same colour as the hair erupting from under the cracked chamber. This mottled black shapeless bolt of cloth ended in battered brogans. Mad blue periwinkle eyes were set in the middle of the 'face' implanted with an iron-hard snout, for rooting in nameless filth. The deep-set eyes were hidden and furtive, wedged into their sockets below the fuzzy eyebrows; the corrugations of the narrow forehead signalling God knows what itch, what fury, puzzlement betraying softly mimed buffoonery with a tug to tow-coloured hair, absented finger up one nostril, a quick tug at the hair wiry as tow, the snot examined and tasted, swallowed. And then stock still, ears cocked, listening hard, then relaxed, whereupon a deep rumbling fart to end this evening's performance. It was a she-beast assuredly to judge from the nauseating vegetable smell that wafted its way across the narrow roadway as we slunk by. Not our Queen Maeve as represented on the one-punt denomination note looking as woebegone as if she had a crippling pain in the hole, nor yet Verfremdungseffekt nor Bubba nor Maggie Humm, nor Banba nor Foohla the Flighty, nor Puckoon, nor the Old-Sow-That-Eats-Her-Farrow, nor yet again Emanrehsihtstahw, the lowly form of an immortal always encountered at that mystical hour 'twixt gloaming and dusk, as now. On all fours, face on fire, grovelling in the dirt.

We passed down the mossy boreen until we came to the main road leading in one direction to nowhere in particular, in the other by the house of hidden Jago and the otter path, then past the flowering cherry at the Carraigin corner and by the blind-factory to the marsh and its assembly of wild birds with their diverse cries, curlews and oystercatchers and plover and mallard, the heavenliness of birdsong that so enraptured W. H. Hudson on the pampas in Argentina in the nineteenth century, as the birds of Hampshire had delighted Gilbert White the Selborne divine in the century before.

The trawler Girl Fiona was tied up at the World's End wharf near where the Cornishman 'mad' Mark Trick lived under a thatched roof with his ever-loving wife Lucinda (née Minogue) of the knockers. Her lord and master was playing loud Magic Flute music all night long on the transistor, having brought his dead mother safely from distant Cornwall in a coffin, set out upon the Harbour Bar counter, Mad Mark calling loudly for drinks on the house. And then the casket up-ended in a corner like a cello, then more drinks before burial in Courtaparteen cemetery, that old disused place near the deserted village.

Only dead fish swim with the tide. Our past is most certainly dead. More than that, much more; it's unimaginable. Unthinkable as the legendary but extinct horseflesh Twohelochroo, or Boggeragh, or flighty Firbolg, or the Pooka, or Babh, or the mighty thundering hooves of the Morrigu herself.

Jackdaws nest in the limes of Friary hill, tear twigs, lay eggs, raise young, drop eggshells and whiten with their squirted lime-shit the newly washed limousines lined up for Mass, strut about on the road. A robin calls 'Swing low, sweet chariot!' over by the French Prison and from near the slaughterhouse on Chairman's Lane a blackbird answers 'Aujourd'hui! Aujourd'hui!' as the legless man is pushed in his wheelchair into a waiting car, and the Buck goes bounding down the narrow stairs and out into the freshness of Cork Street, jacket hooked over one finger, humming 'The Mountains of Mourne', released from rearranging that evergreen lament for his male voice choir.

Daybreak comes early in June to the port, with a bantam cock crowing lustily twenty-nine times, mongrels in the morning, the canoodling of pigeons, the tide coming into the town of ghosts (population 2,000); 1601 was but yesterday, and spooks abound. Joy-bells ring for living and drowned (the Irish life underneath the waves); when the tide goes out and the wind drops there'll be a couple of jumps.

A bitch on heat is being chased through the flat of town by six mongrels anxious to cover her, despite newly enacted by-laws for the control of wandering pets; but ours was ever a country notoriously difficult to control. Windblown pines, surging ambient darkness.

The Battle of Kinsale, from *Hugh*

I must have slept, for I woke to find shafts of pale light coming in around the shutters. I touched his shoulder, "Sir, I must go," and he loosened his hold, and let me rise.

"Wait," he said, when he saw me reaching for the door. "I care not who sees you, I will talk. It is time to finish it." He pulled himself half up, and reached for the little black flask that stood on a press beside the bed. Then he began. "It was the morning of Christmas Eve by the English calendar, January by our own. The storm still drenched us – no weather for man or beast to stir abroad, but we had little choice. An hour or so before dawn O'Donnell peered into my tent, his face pale, his mantle sodden and stained with mud.

"Are you not up yet?" said he, scowling.

"I am as ready as you are," I answered, throwing off my covers. But I was not, none of us were, we were not ready to risk everything on a pitched battle.

He shrugged. "I have come to inform you," he said, choosing his words with cold deliberation, "that I intend to lead our troops today, with my men at the head of the attack."

"You will not," I replied. "This is no mountain skirmish. You have never fought a standing battle, you know nothing of it. I will lead the attack today, your men will follow, and when we engage, they shall come round and sting the enemy in the flank."

O'Donnell's colour rose. "What do you think we are, a straggle of bush-kernes? My men are as skilled at fighting as yours and as courageous. Besides, the English are sleeping, they will be easy to defeat. Last night you had no stomach for this battle. Why should you lead the advance today?"

I had had enough of him, his young-man's petulance. "I am the commander of this army," I roared, "and you will do as I instruct you!"

"I think not!" he threw back at me, stepping out. The tent flap fell back wetly behind him. I shook myself, rubbing my eyes, then climbed out to stretch my stiff limbs. It was almost dawn. In the grey light I saw the rain had lightened a little, though it was misty and there was a strange, still quality to the air. I felt uneasy, there was a sickness in the pit of my stomach, though I was used enough to battle and did not usually suffer so. However I found Tyrrell, and Art O'Hagan with his son Turlough and Mulmore O'Heagarty, and we assembled the men and began to move, as silently as we could, over the ridge beyond our camp, towards the English. The first group of men had just reached the top of the rise when all of a sudden, there came a hissing noise, and with it my skin crawled, as if I had seen a loathsome beast, or a spirit. Then a blue-green flame lit the land around us, and burnt on the men's spears, so each spear-tip seemed a torch. The men cried out in terror, and the horses reared and plunged. As we struggled to control them, O'Donnell spurred up the hill towards me. "What in the Devil's name was that?" I shouted towards him.

"It is a sign from God," he yelled back, "a good omen. I have seen it on board ship, the sailors call it St Elmo's fire, it means protection."

"Protection? Do you think the English sentries have not seen us, after that? Now will you march as I asked you..." But he had ridden back to his men, and was encouraging them. I saw the fool had them marching beside us, so that no-one could taunt him that he had ridden after me. We began to move downwards. After the light there had been a queer pause, but then, just as we began to descend the muddy slope, a most violent and heavy rain fell on us. The horses were slipping, the men ploughing through the mud. As we reached the bottom of the slope the rain lightened a little. The horses were still afraid and difficult to control, but someone knew a pool, so we let them drink, to calm them. A few men filled their porringers and drank too. Then we split up. O'Donnell, still angry, announced that he would go south, towards the Western camp of the English. I went with Tyrrell, O'Sullivan Beare and Del Campo's Spaniards, eastwards to surprise the main camp. I was reluctant to divide our forces, but O'Donnell swore he would meet us before the English could assemble. Besides, he pointed out, Del Aquila's Spaniards would salley out of the town to join us, we would not be short of seasoned men.

After the rain, the mist fell, so thickly that you could not see what was level ground and what was bog, nor any landmarks. Even the scouts seemed unsure of the direction. We crept forwards over the wet grass in an eerie silence, uncertain if we were about to surprise the English, or a herd of cattle. Eventually the ground began to rise. Then the mist lifted a little, and I found myself staring at a troop of horsemen. I thought at first they were Spaniards, come from Kinsale to join us. But when they saw us their red-capped leader shouted, and we saw some musketmen who were with them level their weapons and fire.

"English!" gasped Turlough O'Hagan beside me, as more

horse loomed up – what looked like a whole squadron – and then a long troop of infantry behind them. Some thousand men, or more, in battle order, approaching us. I turned to Turlough, who was staring at them, grey-faced. "Where is Del Aquila, and our reinforcements?" I asked.

"I am not sure" he replied. "The Spaniards said they would sally out as soon as they heard the sounds of battle."

"And where is O'Donnell? Has he come this way, as I told him?"

"Why no, he went farther west, to come around Thomond's camp."

"He went where?" I stared at him. It was at that moment that everything I had worked for seemed to pause, and then begin, like water at the summit of a waterfall, to topple into the chasm. "Find O'Donnell!" I shouted to a scout. The mist lifted further, and we could see two more regiments of the English, assembled in battle order. There was still no sign of the Spanish, so we retreated back over the ford and through a bog to firm ground to wait for them.

Then the squadron began to charge, pounding towards us, driving into the head of our army so that the men in front wavered, then fell back towards the centre. We stumbled against each other, blood spilling from our wounds, the injured obstructing the fresh men. "Mother of God!" I heard one murmur beside me as he sank down, his stomach open. Then more English came around the bog to the rise where we stood, and attacked with horse and foot. I thought we were finished, that we would all die there.

But "O'Neill Abu!" someone cried, and the shout was taken up as 'O'Neill Abu' roared from a hundred throats, and our men fought back and succeeded in turning them. But then more horsemen came over the hill, and attacked our struggling forces in the rear, and this broke us. Our men tried to hold together, but English steel was everywhere, the thick smell of blood filled our nostrils. I roared at the men to stand, my voice cracking, but they could not hear me, they did not know which way to turn. Only the Castlehaven Spanish held their ground, and they were hacked to pieces. The rest took to their heels, utterly routed, and were chased by the English horse along the road. O'Donnell's men never reached us, but fought the Earl of Thomond's Claremen halfway up the hill; some were cut down, the rest ran with the general rout. I retreated with a few followers into the bog, expecting we would join the dead. But the English must have thought it a trap, for they did not pursue us. Then we retreated to Innishannon. The morning of Christ's nativity – and all was lost...

I will not tell you of the fallings out, the leaking of information by spies, the messages going astray, del Aquila's letting down our hopes, so the longed for Spaniards stayed behind their walls and listened – if they heard them at all – to the distant sounds of battle. Nor will I tell you of the recriminations as we crawled away, scattered and unbelieving. All the signs were that we would win – was not God with us, did we not fight His cause? And yet there was a chill round our hearts like a foreboding.

Nor will I list the fruitless letters to Spain, continued though there seemed little hope, because there was nothing else to do but try to milk the diplomacy at which I had once been so skilled. Nor how Mountjoy, with the zeal and fire of a newer world, controlled his men – I had tried to make something like it, or better.

And I had failed."

Tree Ring

The family tree is spread out on the carpet. I kneel on it to flatten the greaseproof paper. My youngest brother put the tree together two decades ago. But why greaseproof – unwieldy, crackling in my hands and hard on the knees? 'It was the nearest to parchment I could find.' Now it needs updating. New births, marriages and deaths. I buy Stephen's ink and a fountain pen. My brother's hand is neat and tidy. After all, he was writing for posterity.

The entries are a pyramid with hieroglyphics, the names and dates. At the pinnacle is Edmund Hogan, my great-great-great-grandfather (born 1713), a Catholic farmer in the bleakest province in Ireland. Cromwell banished the native gentry there – 'to hell or Connaught'. After ethnic cleansing, ethnic conflict. The dispossessed scrambled for land. Edmund's father came up with good land in a barren county. The family motto is 'Fulminis Instar' ('Like Lightning').

I scan for patterns. In the eighteenth and nineteenth centuries, one member in each generation has a large family. Usually the eldest son who inherited the land. Occasionally the daughter – marrying a local farmer. In Penal times

Catholic families had no access to the professions. So the rest of the children had the choice between a new life in America or an ecclesiastical career.

The majority went for the Church, where the family did well on the Continent (founders of seminaries, confessors to princesses, reverend mothers). The American few disappeared into the modest middle class or lower. Zane Grey in his Westerns often chose the name Hogan for ignominious hangers-on.

Catholic Emancipation offered the Law as an alternative. Usually the eldest son took it up but only as a sideline. My grandfather exemplified this, becoming the Chief Inspector in Parnell's Land League. He returned absentee estates to the native Irish. His sons and daughters emerged, an educated elite from the bogs. They took the National University by storm. Idealists, intellectuals, sportsmen and cultured hostesses. The secularisation of the family came with them and the new Free State. Five large families resulted and the diaspora began. Later than most – the family had stayed put and together despite famines. Their children and their children's children secured a wide base of offspring, spread over four continents. The pyramid's collapse into the splits continues.

Tagging the tree for the next generation is disheartening. So many branches have twigs that disappear into nothing, lost to a larger world. It is like visiting a cemetery of unmarked graves. I revert to calculating life spans. Is there a trend? Spinsters and bachelors were long-lived, married males died young. I clutch my heart.

Numbers reoccur. My grandfather was twenty-four when his father died. He died at forty-five, my father was twenty-one. I was twenty-one when my father died. That was twenty-four years ago. Twenty-four year circles loop the generations. Has the cycle been broken? I do not have a son.

Playing with numbers is a game of impatience. I force imperatives on the past with opportunistic sums. I want to see the back of it. Number up. Line ended. Full stop.

The antithesis to numbers is ideas. I meditate upon the pattern of the hieroglyphics. What is a pyramid? An apex sloping to a polygonal base, a burial pile for royal stock. Redundant now. My generation is urban middle class. Our lives and ashes scattered to the four winds in four continents, unconfined. My ancestors are dust immured in a pyramid of calligraphy. The family motto 'Like Lightning' – flash!

Family trees only have significance when related to land. And land for us is limited to the gardens around our houses. The snakes and ladders of life's extremities – birth and death (marriage is no longer an immutable) – patterned before me is a game for dodos.

The collapsed pyramid has been paved over by a patio.

I fold the document into a jiffy bag. Something is wrong. If it is not already obvious to the reader I am forgiven. My family tree, for what it is worth, has been split in half. One half – my father's – is branched with nametags budding births, flowering marriages and berrying deaths. The other half – my mother's – lacking records, is in invisible ink. Which makes it a tree you can hang anything you like on. Gifts from oral memory, dreams and historical possibilities.

Turn on the lights.

Spanish sailors from the Armada shipwrecked off Kinsale. Bodies are swept on to the rocks. The locals have heard portents of princes rising from the sea with bags of sovereigns on their backs. They look on – helpless till the storm dies down. Then they assemble the corpses on the beach, stripping them of gold and other valuables. Till they come upon the Galician. Alive. He flickers a smile.

Sheltering Spaniards means death by the spike. He is just

a boy, but smart – when they whisper 'Imirt has' he played dead. The Redcoats watch as he is carried ashore covered in kelp and dumped in the cart with the dead. But on the blind side. When the cart jolts off, the College is caped into a cabin. 'Who are you?' the woman of the house asks. 'Yo soy Gallego.' He is taken care of. Gallegos are the Celts of Spain, small, dark, sharp, and hard working. They travel well. In no time the boy becomes one of them. Speaks their language, finds his place. They call him Gal Ghaoithe (Blast of Warm Wind). Haifa Gaelic transliteration of his tribe. Haifa tribute to the gale that threw him up. In time he will prosper as a tanner, his father's trade.

Thirteen years later the Great O'Neill marches from Ulster to Kinsale. Over three hundred miles. The Spanish expeditionary force lead by Don Juan del Aquila has arrived. But is under siege in Kinsale (Gal makes himself useful as an interpreter between the town and the Don). The British are one step ahead. Something O'Neill in his pride and contempt overlooks. He attacks Mountjoy's army in the wrong place at the wrong time and is routed. And retreats north ignominiously.

A little girl becomes separated from the O'Neill straggle. Gal spots her weeping in a ditch. She is the daughter of a dead soldier. Gives her name as Una O'Neill. He puts Una under his protection. Takes her to his workshop. Looks after her. Marries her. Assumes her name Gal O'Neill.

Centuries later in Orense I sat in a cafe watching the youngsters sucking their milkshakes. A dark determined little lady with corrugated jet black hair, practical hands and a remote look took my order. It was my mother. During my month in Galicia I met my mother many times in various guises. I was home. Some soldiers from Aquila's force remain on. Mostly from the Celtic North. Stone masons, carpenters, men with trades that built the great cathedrals of the north-east of Spain. Salamanca, Santiago de Compostela. They see in Kinsale the makings of a Spanish town, a pocket Vigo. The headland descends into narrow winding arched lanes on a hilly plateau. Ochre earth, red slate and the ocean beyond. These men of Galicia helped shape the only Spanish town in Ireland today.

The Gallego O'Neills graft a tolerable living in Kinsale. Skilful people. When the tannery falls foul of the occupying British – fearful of sabotage, imported their own artisans – the O'Neills turn their hand to building granaries for local farmers. Their style is distinctive, based on the Galician horreo. Mushroom-like stores raised on stone platforms to protect the grain from rats. When bailiffs, fearful of sabotage, increasingly employ army craftsmen they turn to thatching cabins. A thatched cabin is a cottage, a status symbol for tenant farmers. Calls for thatching lessened with the famines of the mid-nineteenth century. The O'Neills moonlight as migrant workers on conacres. These tenant cooperatives offer a seasonal living for hordes of willing hands in hard times. All the same, thatching is a skill that survived into this century. My mother's father was the last in line.

The sixth child in thatchers' families are born with a sixth finger on their left hand. That is the legend. Watching my mother putting up a light bulb or climbing through a skylight, I knew she was a thatcher's daughter.

The Gallego O'Neills never tenanted land for long. They were too honest to cheat the rent collectors. When the Land League came their hopes were high. But a local gombeen man duped them of their due. This was not uncommon. My mother's father did not live long enough to see things otherwise. Providing for eleven children through farm labouring and thatching is hard. One year he diversified into cramming turkeys for Christmas. My mother coming home from school saw them perched in the barnyard trees.

The birds could not be coaxed down. The turkey dream came to nothing. My maternal grandfather died in his forties. He never thatched his own cabin.

The eldest sister took over the family. Already she was in a position of some prestige, the parish priest's housekeeper. Most of the brothers emigrated and lived decent lives in jobs requiring manual skills.

My mother was seen as the daughter most likely to marry into land. Petite, olive skinned. Darkly pretty. Quick at school. Strong legs and hands. At sixteen the priest found her a job in a city guesthouse. Here she would learn nice, domestic ways to increase her eligibility. My father, a bachelor professor, took rooms with service.

He is attempting to teach the landlady's boy the rudiments of arithmetic. My mother knocks and enters, sees the bemusement of the boy. Tells my father off and explains vulgar fractions in simple terms. The boy understands. He approached the parish priest and offered to finance my mother's renewed education. She was sent to the nuns in Fermoy. The eldest sister, disappointed in her plans, declared the girl a kept woman and cut her off. That was that. My mother's mother met her secretly from time to time. It was a great sorrow for her and the other siblings.

She was excluded from her mother's deathbed.

My mother's father's brother was a musician and took life easy. He lived to see his children prosper. Owning not only land (through my mother's younger sister's marriage), but the local garage, pub and shop. Recently an unmarried grandson opened a gourmet restaurant. Meals cooked by hand, his own. Most of my generation and their children still live in Kinsale. My mother's Gallego looks survive in two of her children, my younger brother and second sister. The Gal O'Neill line is fertile. I look at the hands of the grandchildren. Artisan potential, a sixth finger?

This is the other half of the tree as told to me.

Gal Ghaoithe meets Fulminis Instar. Lightning strikes, warm winds balm.

Alannah Hopkin

The Sleakin Monument

Sleakin is all up and down.

Seapoint and Tresco are at the extremities of its crescent-shaped harbour, linked by a series of quays. From the sea, the view of Sleakin is dominated by the Castle Hill, steep and conical with a ruined castle on top. Behind the seafront narrow streets run off at unexpected angles creating wide spaces when five or six roads converge. The local people use hidden steps and steep paths which only the most inquisitive visitor will find. There are many visitors in the summer months, some of them following the recommendation of Sleakin's eminent historian Professor Prionsias O' Tierniagh and taking 'a leisurely stroll through the time-worn by-ways of Sleakin'. In spite of the map in his booklet, most of the visitors are soon lost.

If you walk out of town heading around Castle Hill you suddenly find yourself in open country. Just as suddenly, you are back into town again, not the town you have just left with large Georgian houses set in spacious gardens looking out to sea, but a sheltered inland village, a gentle hill lined with terraced cottages painted in bright, often clashing colours, more Mediterranean than Irish. This part of Sleakin is called Ballinalea.

There are three distinct Sleakin accents. At the Mills and in the flat of town-the main commercial areas – they talk very fast and emphasise words in unexpected places: 'Cauliflowers are down today, *praise* be to God.' says Katy the plump greengrocer to Sister Imelda. 'They're a bargain now, in *all* fairness.' Travel to Seapoint, a hundred yards by water, half a twisty mile by road, and you could be out west with the slower, more guttural sing-song voices: 'We'll have one more pint and then we'll go home for the tea.'

Seapoint and the flat of town both laugh at Tresco, where the influence of the Cornish fishermen who settled there in the last century can still be heard in vowels that belong in the west of England and a strange way with their haitches. The rest of the town mimics Tresco by saying 'They 'ang their 'at on the 'ook in the 'all and when they're sick they go hup to the 'awspiddel'. A Tresco man who says hoak, hash and helm is talking about trees.

Sleakin people have a highly localised sense of civic pride: everyone believes that their corner of town is superior to everyone else's. Up on the Castle Hill they look down on the people who live in the flat of the town. The new bungalows in Knockatee overlook the back of the

Castle Hill. They are proud of their ranch-style homes, and pity the Castle Hill dwellers' draughty Georgian houses. The flat of town looks down on Ballinalea above it in view of the sea and an uphill walk home with the messages. Ballinalea people know that Ballinalea is the most sheltered and the most neighbourly part of town, and therefore the best. Nobody wants to live at the Mills because they all know it is haunted, and the stink of the slaughterhouse doesn't help. But the people of the Mills would never move to any other part of town, especially not Seapoint or Tresco which they only grudgingly admit to be part of Sleakin at all. Everyone looks down on Seapoint and Tresco, and Seapoint and Tresco look down on each other, glaring steadily across the harbour.

'They're not the full shilling in Tresco,' they say in Seapoint.

'They're hall 'alf bats hover in Seapoint,' you'll be told in Tresco.

The only disadvantage that all residents of Sleakin will admit to, whatever part of town they live in, is that they cannot get good reception on multi-channel television, no matter how many aerials and gadgets they buy. If you plan to watch multi-channel in Sleakin of an evening, you must listen to the weather forecast at noon. The only chance of reasonable reception, and then not always reliable, is during high atmospheric pressure. If a low is coming in from the Atlantic, you'll have to make other plans.

The Mills and the flat of the town, Seapoint and Tresco, the Castle Hill, Knockatee and Ballinalea were formed into an Urban District in the late nineteenth century. Certain decisions are taken in Sleakin by the elected members of the Urban District Council at their monthly meeting in Sleakin's Courthouse under the chairmanship of Owen MacCarthy.

At last week's meeting, these eight good men and true, approved, in principle, seven for and one against, the Government's offer to erect a monument in Sleakin's town park to celebrate Sleakin's success in a competition to discover the most picturesque port in Europe.

Sleakin came twenty-fifth out of sixty two, a great victory for Ireland, and for a town of Sleakin's modest size and resources. The town would have come much higher, according to the judges' comments, had it not been for the individualistic style of bungalow and chalet preferred by the inhabitants of Seapoint and Tresco, the dilapidation of the old Georgian properties on the Castle Hill and the plastic windows and front doors in the Georgian house that had been done up (there is no pleasing some people, said Owen MacCarthy). The judges also remarked unfavourably on the clashing colours of the cottages at Ballinalea (an ancient seafaring tradition which one might have expected the eminent judges to be aware of, said Professor Prionsias O' Tierniagh) and complained about the ornate Californian-style facades of the bungalows at Knockatee and the plastic and neon signs that have sprouted all over the Mills and in the flat of town.

Marks were lost over such minor quibbles, but Sleakin scored high marks for the natural beauty of its harbour, the wild flowers that grew in its open spaces, and the clear, unpolluted waters around it.

The Urban District Council, having approved, in principle, to accept the Government's offer to erect a monument in the town park on the sea front, then agreed, in principle, seven for and one against, to hold a public meeting with the people that they represented, to discuss what form such a monument should take. The abstainer, a dour Tresco man, stubbornly refused to acknowledge that there was hanything to celebrate in coming twenty-fifth out of sixty two.

Public meetings in Sleakin are always well-attended, and the monument meeting was no exception. The whole town was there: all eight members of the Urban District Council, most of the twenty seven publicans, the two doctors and their wives, the Parish priest and the Rector of St. Blecan's, the Foreman of the Board of Works, the President of the G.A.A., members of the Historical, Gardening and Dramatic Societies and a good sprinkling of blow-ins.

The Chairman Owen MacCarthy read out the first suggestion. It was an official communication from the County Architect: 'The Sleakin monument shall consist of a large corton steel structure to be commissioned by the Arts Council from an award-winning sculptor which will reflect and enhance Sleakin's unique maritime environment.'

In other words, modern art.

This was rejected without discussion. Nobody wanted anything to do with modern art.

A Seapoint man suggested a memorial in local granite to all Sleakin men lost at sea. This was seconded by a Tresco voice and seemed to have general approval. Then Professor Prionsias O' Tierniagh pointed out that there were already two such memorials, one in Seapoint and one in Tresco, and both were in a bad state of neglect. Why not, he said, restore these monuments to their former glory and put something else in the town park?

Miss Warren of the Castle Hill caught Owen Macarthy's eye. He begged silence, then Miss Warren, a tweedy, birdlike woman much respected by her peers, revealed her plan: an ecumenical monument to the patron saint of Sleakin.

Her phrasing was a masterpiece of diplomacy. Sometime between the sixth and the twelfth century, Teáth's name was changed to Blectan. So obscure is the town's patron that nobody is sure if the saint is male or female. The thirteenth century Protestant church is called St. Blectans; the Catholic graveyard, on the site of a much earlier religious foundation, is called St. Teáth's.

Miss Warren's suggestion provoked a long and animated discussion. Canon Moore of St. Blectan's feared that, for all its good intentions, such a monument might emphasise differences rather than reconciliation. His parishioners saw St. Blectan as a man, while the Parish Priest's flock was convinced that St. Teáth was a woman. St. Teáth was indeed a woman, said Father Hogan P.P.. Professor O' Tierniagh confirmed that Blectan and Teáth were definitely the same person, but he could not help to determine the sex: there were good arguments for both in his opinion as a historian.

A blow-in suggested an androgynous figure. There was an uproar. The people of Sleakin, who were born in Sleakin and reared in Sleakin, and intended, when the time came, to die in Sleakin, were not having anything androgynous in their town. They all know where that sort of thing might lead.

Owen MacCarthy called the meeting to order, and produced a compromise: instead of an ecumenical monument, which presented insuperable difficulties, would Canon Moore and Father Hogan agree to hold an ecumenical dedication for a secular monument something similar to last week's ecumenical dedication of the Bottle Bank on Giles's Quay?

Swayed by the warm applause that greeted the chairman's suggestion, the reverend gentlemen agreed.

Owen MacCarthy then called for an uncontroversial suggestion, and Seamus Harrington of Ballinalea proposed an ornamental stone fountain on a paved podium surrounded by flower beds. There was a murmur of approval, but no great excitement.

Owen had a reputation for fairness. 'We haven't heard at all from Knockatee,' he said. 'Is there anyone from Knockatee with a word to say?'

Jerry Byrne, a computer salesman who owned the

biggest bungalow in Knockatee spoke up.

'In all fairness now, chairman, as the Professor has pointed out, Sleakin is crawling with monuments, the whole town is a monument, a relic of the past, which is all very well for bringing in the tourists, but we don't need another monument. What we do need, as I think everyone will agree, is a decent television aerial to serve the whole community and bring us into the twenty-first century...'

Up at the Pier Head, exactly one hour after high tide, several hundred tons of Soya nuts from West Africa are being unloaded on to waiting lorries from the Lydia, a coaster out of Rotterdam under a Panamanian flag, crewed by Laskars. A light drizzle is falling.

On Lobster Quay in Tresco, men with hard blue faces and knitted woollen hats are spreading orange fishing nets on the tarmac. Miss Warren of the Castle Hill passes by with two Prince Charles spaniels on leads, taking a constitutional as far as the Archdeacon Henry Boylan Bridge.

In a small house mid-way between the flat of town and Ballinalea the Sleakin Correspondent of the Atlantic Eagle is biting his pencil as he selects appropriate words to describe the Ecumenical Dedication of the Sleakin Monument.

"This auspicious event was witnessed by several representatives of both religious communities in spite of inclement weather..."

The Sleakin Monument, which stands in the town park on the seafront, looks like a replica Eiffel Tower topped by a flying saucer. Television reception in Sleakin is now excellent in all weathers. A plaque in front of it says: "In Commemoration of Sleakin's Success in the Picturesque European Ports Competition, July 1987. Ecumenically dedicated by Father J.D.Hogan, P.P. and Canon E.F. Moore, Rector, on July 24, 1988."

In the summer months the Sleakin Monument is surrounded by a brightly coloured display of marigolds and petunias.

Notes on the Authors

James Clarence Mangan was born in 1803 and was a hugely influential poet and translator. However, since his death in 1849 much of his work was out of print until recently.

Thomas Davis wrote essays, ballads and poems advocating Irish nationalism including *A Nation Once Again*. He was born in Mallow, Co. Cork in 1814 and died of scarlatina in 1845.

Aubrey de Vere, 1814 -1902, was a poet and critic of English rule in Ireland, particularly during the Famine. He also published travel writings, books on religion, legends and written portraits of his many friends.

Austin Clarke was born in Dublin in 1896. He was a journalist, poet and novelist. His poetry was heavily influenced by classical Irish language poetry. He died in 1974.

Desmond O'Grady was born in Limerick in 1935. He has published numerous books of poetry including both a *Collected Poems* and *Collected Translations*. He lives in Kinsale.

John Montague, born in Brooklyn in 1929, was the first Ireland Professor of Poetry. His publications include *The Rough Field*, *The Dead Kingdom* and *Collected Poems*.

Derek Mahon has won numerous awards for both poetry and translation. He was born in Belfast in 1941 and currently resides in Kinsale. His books include *The Yellow Book*, *The Hudson Letter* and *Collected Poems*.

Matthew Geden was born and brought up in the English Midlands. He moved to Kinsale in 1990 and has since published poems in numerous magazines and journals. His *Kinsale Poems* and *Autumn: Twenty Poems by Guillaume Apollinaire* were published by Lapwing.

Criose Brogan is a poet, playwright and novelist. She spent many years in London before moving to Kinsale over twenty years ago.

Afric Hamilton is a poet and journalist who moved to Kinsale from Zimbabwe. Her reviews and articles appear regularly in the *Irish Examiner*.

Gabriel Ezutah was born in Nigeria in 1965. His first collection of poems *Pebbles of Sound* was published by Trafford Publishing.

Michael Hamburger was born in Berlin in 1924. He is well known as a poet, translator and critic. His *Collected Poems* were published in 1995.

Catriona Ryan is a poet and playwright from Ballina, Co. Mayo. She has been previously published in anthologies including *Women's Works IX* as part of the 1999 International Women's Poetry Competition.

Lennox Robinson, 1886-1958, was born in Douglas, Co. Cork. He was best known for his many plays including *The Big House* and *Drama at Inish*. He also wrote autobiographies, short stories and political sketches.

Robert Gibbings was born in Cork in 1889 and died in 1958. He was an artist, book-designer and travel writer. He was heavily influenced by the artist and lithographer Eric Gill.

Maureen Murphy, 1914-1991, a niece of Lennox Robinson, lived much of her early life in India but was schooled in Ireland. In *A Child of Two Continents* she recalls this time with particularly fond memories of Sandycove, near Kinsale.

Aidan Higgins, born in 1927, is one of Ireland's foremost prose writers. His novels include *Langrishe, Go Down* and *Balcony of Europe*, whilst he has also written short stories and an autobiography *A Bestiary*.

Rosemary Canavan was born in Scotland, but is presently living in County Cork. She has written children's books, poetry and a novel *Hugh* based upon the life of Hugh O'Neill.

Augustus Young was born in Cork in 1943. He has written plays, poetry and most recently a book of prose memoirs entitled *Light Years*. He is currently living in France.

Alannah Hopkin is a short-story writer, novelist and journalist living in Kinsale. She regularly contributes articles and reviews to *The Irish Times* and *The Irish Examiner*.

Acknowledgements

For their support and encouragement we would like to thank Desmond O'Grady, Gerry Wrixon, John Minihan, Hammond Journeaux, Liz Willows, Máire Bradshaw, Stinging Fly Magazine, Alan Murray, Dennis and Rene Greig, Patrick Galvin, Mary Johnson, John Shinnors, Patrick Cotter, Gabriel Rosenstock, Jack Donovan, Oliver Flynn, Rob Jacob, Carole Norman, Eugene Gillan, Adam Wyeth, Kerry Naber, Tony Boland, Mark Whelan, Foras na Gaeilge, Aidan Higgins, Alannah Hopkin, Fintan Lynch, Maureen Tierney, Dermot Ryan, Adrian Wistreich, Ashley Cavers, Colleen O'Sullivan, Eugene O' Connell, Sally-Ann Attale and Seamus O'Mahony. Also thanks to all who submitted work. A personal thank you from Barry Moloney and Matthew Geden to their families.

Anam Press have made every effort to trace the copyright holders of the work in this anthology. We will happily correct any errors or omissions in future editions or reprints. Grateful acknowledgement is made to the following; Desmond O' Grady for *Kinsale*, *Dún Chearmna* and *The Manuscripts of Louis MacNeice* published in *The Road Taken: Poems 1956-1996* by University of Salzburg Press. John Montague for *After Kinsale, 1604* published in *Collected Poems* by Gallery Press. Derek Mahon for *Birdlife*, *On the Automation of the Irish Lights*, *Christmas in Kinsale* and *Kinsale* published in *Collected Poems* by Gallery Press. Matthew Geden for *Ghost Story* published in *Kinsale Poems* by Lapwing Press. Criose Brogan for *Irish Exile*, Afric Hamilton for *The Discovery of Kinsale*, Catriona Ryan for *The Robin*, Michael Hamburger and Anvil Press for *To a Fellow Poet* published in *Collected Poems 1941-1994*, Gabriel Ezutah for *Demands of Life*, Aidan Higgins for *Sodden Fields* which is an extract from *Flotsam & Jetsam*, Rosemary Canavan for *The Battle of Kinsale*, from *Hugh*, Augustus Young for *Tree Ring* from *Light Years* published by London Magazine Editions and Alannah Hopkin for *The Sleakin Monument*.